Alisha,
Best Wishes and
to You Always

Love
[signature]

July 3, 2000

The Voice for Feminine Responsible Living

I want to hear from you. Please email your comments to:

drsusiehill@sbcglobal.net

My Secret Weapon: Unlocking the Explosive Inner Power of a Woman
Copyright © 2010 by Susie M. Hill

Helping Hands Press
P.O. Box 380941
Duncanville, Texas 75138
214.673.9434

Library of Congress Cataloging-in-Publication Data
Hill, Susie M.
    My Secret Weapon: Unlocking the Explosive Inner Power of a Woman/
    Dr. Susie M. Hill
    p. cm.
    ISBN # 1-889390-11-9
    1. Women's Issues   2. Christian Life   3. Christian Culture
    I. Title
    BR 2010904381

All Scripture quotations, unless otherwise noted, are taken from the New King
James Version, copyright © 1979, 1980, 1982 by Thomas Nelson, Inc.

Edited by **Roland J. Hill, Kenneth Hall, Patricia Humphrey**
Cover Design by **Jerry Ross Design**
Hair Styling by **James McCarter**
Make-up by **Jackie Wood**
Book Layout by **3Ring Design Studio**
Art Illustrations by **Julie Stoker**

Dedication

I dedicate this book to all women who courageously fight to leave a positive impact on the world for Christ through their Explosive Inner Power.

My Secret Weapon

"In like manner also, that the women adorn themselves in
modest apparel, with propriety and moderation, not with
braided hair or gold or pearls or costly clothing, but, which
is proper for women professing godliness, with good works."
(1 Timothy 2: 9, 10)

Table of Contents

Acknowledgements

There are so many women who have had a profound impact on my life that it is difficult to name them all. First of all, I am so grateful to you, Mom (Mavis Smith), for demonstrating what it means to live as a responsible woman, caring for the needs of your children without compromising your feminine power. Your enduring, tireless strength, your commitment to hard work, and consistent exercise are matchless. Although it is not one of my favorite things to do, you taught me how to get in the kitchen and prepare a hot meal in minutes. Thanks for everything, Mom! Secondly, I am also grateful for life lessons learned sitting at the feet of my mother-in-law, Lucille Hill. You have been like a mother to me in every way. Your wisdom, encouragement, and support have shaped my secret weapon profoundly.

I am also thankful to the women from the 31st Street

Seventh-day Adventist Church for looking out for me during my adolescent years. This is the church where I was baptized and married. It was the women in this church who allowed me, as a young girl, to find my way in life by letting me play the piano for the worship services and deliver my first sermon. Thank you, Vivian Stokes, for showing me through your life, now as an octogenarian, that a woman can grow and develop with beauty and style across one's lifespan. I still have the fine china you selected and gave me as a wedding gift 35 years ago. Dr. Rowena Armster, my former high school teacher, you may not know it, but you have shown me and the world that a woman's happiness is determined by taking her feminine power and seizing every opportunity that comes her way.

After completing my first year of college, I decided that nursing was not for me. On registration day of my sophomore year, I was frustrated because I did not know which major to declare. Dr. Maxine Taylor, from the Home Economics Department (now called Family Consumer Sciences), piqued my interest by describing Home Economics as the only field of study designed to preserve families, so I said, "Sign me up." Thank you so much for the spark that has ignited into a blaze.

It was not until I was about to complete my coursework

for my doctorate that my life went through yet another transformation through my experience at Texas Woman's University (TWU). Three women taught me life lessons that were catalysts for writing this book. Dr. Mary Bold, you taught me that "your minimums become your maximums." Thank you for teaching me this, because setting high goals is now the standard for me. Dr. Lillian Cheneweth, I learned from you the importance of going beneath the surface. This is the lesson that shook me at the very core of my being. It was a painful lesson, but I certainly love the results. I would not have made it through the most grueling course of study that I have ever undertaken without the guidance of my major advisor, Dr. Joyce Armstrong. Thank you for being approachable and patient, and for giving me the three words that pushed me: "Just do it."

I also want to thank you, Dr. Myrtle Glascoe, my friend, for setting a high standard by completing your Ph.D. when it was not popular for women. I admire your wit and your brilliance as a mother, educator, and community activist.

Although some of the women who have made a profound impact in my life are no longer living, I am forever grateful for their influence in my life. Before going off to college, little did I know that the many meals I was served in the home of the late Sylvia Canson, wife of the former Pastor Earl Canson, would be the precursor of a life of ministry through hospitality. I really thought that every minister's wife prepared and served dinner for guests each week. Then, I will always remember the late Dr. Frances Mosely, former professor at Southwestern Adventist University. She was such an inspiration to me. Dr. Mosely was a woman of principle and fine character; her feminine power touched my heart and inspired me to appreciate being a woman. These are only a few of the women who have paved the way for me to use my explosive inner power.

I must add that it was not only women who helped to shape my life; there are also a few men who made a difference. I know that God sent you, Dr. Larry Leflore, as department chair of Family Sciences at TWU, to speak words into my life when I came to your office to withdraw from a challenging class. I was telling myself, "The teacher is going to fail me, I just know that the teacher is going to fail me." And you said, "You must change the messages that you are giving yourself." Little did I know how those negative messages were about to destroy me. I changed those negative messages, and the outcome of that change is awesome. Thank you. You saved my life!

But I certainly would not be the woman that I am today without the love, patience, encouragement, and support that

Acknowledgements

I have received from my husband, Roland. Thank you for loving me the same way God loves me, unconditionally. I love you for that. I would be remiss if I didn't thank the staff of the Helping Hands Press for the spirit of excellence they brought to this project. And finally, I give all praises to God for directing my life and giving me the privilege to have an impact for His Kingdom.

– Dr. Susie M. Hill

Foreword

Woman was the crowning act of creation. She was perfect in every detail and an ideal companion to man, complementing him in a healthy, holy way. God gave woman special powers which, when used as He intended, bless and elevate society. Since the beginning, however, woman has been the object of Satan's most insidious attacks. In too many cases he has been successful in convincing women that the special gifts God gave them are worthless.

Women who don't understand the value of their God-given gifts don't respect themselves as befitting daughters of the King. This is often evidenced by mindlessly following fashion to the point of totally ignoring basic principles of modesty. Fashion doesn't dictate modesty, and when fashion deviates from Christian principles, it must be rejected, not embraced.

Foreword

One of the special gifts God gave women is purity — not just sexual purity, but purity of thought, action, and influence. The women of the church have a sacred responsibility to guard not only our own purity, but that of our girls and young women — and also of our boys and men. Since we know that men are aroused visually, modern Eves should be concerned with helping Christian men keep their thoughts and actions pure.

Obviously, society is working against us. Television, magazines, and every other medium promote immodesty and promiscuity. But Christians should not give up the fight. Someone must hold up godly standards, and if the women of the church capitulate, the battle is lost for generations.

That's why I have been especially pleased with Dr. Susie Hill's seminars and now her book addressing the almost-lost ideals of Christian modesty and purity. Satan has convinced many women that these belong to a bygone era and have no place in the 21st century. But Christian principles are timeless. Yes, fashions change, but each new trend must be weighed against eternal principles.

Dr. Hill has done an excellent job of identifying the issues and giving practical ways to test one's appearance and clothing to ensure that they conform to these eternal principles. It is still possible to dress both fashionably and modestly. I believe Dr. Hill's insights will reignite a desire in Christian women to use their God-given gifts as a blessing to themselves and others as they seek to glorify God in their bodies.

– Carla Baker
Women's Ministries Director
North American Division of Seventh-day Adventists

Introduction

I'm like every other woman; I like to feel good and look good when I go out. It's a natural part of who I am. I have always sought to confidently project who I am and who I would like to become, but honestly, I wonder at times, Am I effectively conveying the message of who I am? As a pastor's wife, professor, and seminar presenter, I have seen many women join me in the struggle to know who we are and become confident about our feminine identity. Expressing our femininity in ways that truly communicate who we are is a major battle waged by women in the 21st century. In the white heat of this battle, I am now more keenly aware than ever of the role of dress in expressing our femininity and will in this book share with you my discoveries about dress. But this is not a book about dress. This is a book about *being*. It is about the awareness of who we are as women. It is about reaffirming that we are extraordinary creations of God with explosive inner power. Reflecting on our beginnings, the biblical account of creation describes women as having positional power: "And the Lord God caused a deep sleep to fall on Adam, and he slept; and He took one of his ribs, and closed up the flesh in its place. Then the rib which the Lord God had taken from man He made into a woman, and He brought her to the man. And Adam said: 'This is now bone of my bones and flesh of my flesh; She shall be called Woman, because she was taken out of Man'" (Genesis 2:21-23). This was "the position which God originally designed for her, as her husband's equal."[1] We women came from the hand of God with equal position and power. However, history records mixed messages about the position and role of women in society. The story of women, since the original sin, has been the painful struggle of women seeking to regain their rightful place in society. It shows women under the feet of men rather than by their side. This painful and often oppressive saga has left us women uncertain about our feminine identity.

In colonial times, women were in charge of running and operating the home. But during that same period, women were expected to refrain from doing any work outside of the home. Women were not allowed to hold public office or perform any outdoor manual labor. However, the domestic duties that were performed by colonial women in the home were constant and more challenging than some of the manual outdoor labor. The duties of one colonial mother with fourteen children showed that she engaged in "candle making, soap making, butter and cheese making, spinning, weaving, dyeing and of course, all the knitting, sewing, dressmaking, and tailoring."[2] That's a lot of work. The women in those days were indeed tremendous helpmeets to their husbands. Women lived their lives like this for centuries. A man would boast, "I keep my wife barefoot and pregnant," as a paradoxical expression of control and admiration of the power of a woman. That was a woman's place.

In the 1920s, during the first wave of feminism, women in America began challenging the traditional views and roles of women. Women no longer saw themselves as second-class citizens whose jobs were just to stay at home, bear children, and be a domestic for men. Their explosive inner power was felt in new ways when women finally were given the right to vote. But it was not until the second wave of feminism in the 1970s that women experienced a complete change in their roles and their feminine power was released beyond the home. Women went to work outside of the home in droves. Prior to the second feminist movement, only 30 percent of women worked outside of the home; after this second wave, the numbers increased to 70 percent.[3] Betty Friedan, in her book, *The Feminine Mystique*, is credited with igniting the contemporary women's movement.[4] During the 1960s, the civil unrest was felt in the home as women voiced their negative sentiments at being stay-at-home moms. Friedan released women to think beyond their traditional roles by awakening them to their value in society and helping them feel good about being a woman. Friedan gave women the courage to step out and work alongside their male counterparts.[5]

The feminist movement, while often misunderstood as only being concerned about women, saw this era as an opportunity to shed light on women's experiences, in hopes of creating an equal society for all human beings.[6] Others saw the civil unrest of the 1960s as an opportunity for women to gain power. For them, a woman's identity was no longer rooted in or limited to the role of being a wife or mother but her role now was to be a power broker helping shape modern society.[7] This liberation movement among women performed an important role on the journey to self-discovery. But it failed in helping us re-discover our power. The movement called for women to pursue power outside of ourselves. It taught us to see power externally and not internally. Therefore, the emphasis was directed toward rights, not virtue, toward something earned, not an inborn gift. As the "voice for feminine responsible living," my purpose in this book is to ignite your explosive inner power. I am committed to teaching you that the power you so greatly desire you already have. You were born with it! You are "awesome!" Eve, our original mother, came from the hand of God imprinted with position and power. She demonstrated to us the magnitude of her feminine power in the famous and fatal episode in the garden with Adam. You are a daughter of Eve. You were born with explosive inner power. You didn't earn it. You don't deserve it. It is a gift of God.

Every woman needs to discover her explosive inner power. But after years in the power struggle and watching other women in the struggle, experience has taught me that knowing that we have power isn't enough. Women need to know how to use their power. The explosive inner power of women is not a toy. It isn't a low-voltage battery or a dull butter knife. It is a highly explosive weapon. That's why I have entitled this book *My Secret Weapon*. As the voice for feminine responsible living, I see the proper use of this weapon as critical to the survival of the home, the church, and society. My job is to teach women how to properly use this awesome power. Each page of this book is designed to inspire, motivate, and educate women to experience feminine responsible living, to teach women how to use their weapon for the benefit of mankind and for the glory of God. I will teach from three lenses: theology, social theory, and common sense. Theology gives us the biblical foundation for living. It is God's manual that gives instructions about the explosive inner power of women. Through precepts and portraits, we learn God's methods for using this powerful gift. The biblical lens is a must in an age when the classroom for learning about feminine responsible living is Hollywood, not the holy halls of the church. Therefore, I have been intentional about developing biblical standards for living through examining different ways women in the Bible used their explosive inner power.

While the theological lens provides the foundation for living, social theory provides an opportunity to frame the concept for understanding the explosive inner power of a woman. It provides research-based findings that allow us to discuss what the issues are in the struggle of feminine power and its use. *My Secret Weapon* uses the theoretical rationale of phenomenology and gestalt theory to guide the discussion as I unlock the explosive inner power of a woman as seen through the topics of modesty, fashion, and the "secret weapon."

As a family scientist, I have discovered that common sense is not so common in today's world. Therefore, I have adopted common-sense measures that you can use to assist you as you take responsibility for your feminine power. This is the nuts and bolts. This is where the rubber meets the road. This is the real test of feminine responsible living. These simple guides are for your use. Please don't use them to become the fashion police for other women. Instead, as you take seriously the use of your secret weapon, you will inspire other women to do the same. Let every woman say – Amen!

– Dr. Susie M. Hill

My Secret Weapon

"We women were born with explosive inner power. We didn't earn it. We don't deserve it. It is a gift of God."

– Dr. Susie M. Hill

My Secret Weapon

Chapter One
The Power

Power? I really didn't know I had power. What do house-wives know about power, anyway? I stayed home in the early years of marriage to raise my children and take care of the house and my husband. Power was something that did not cross my mind. I had a job to do. You know, "a mother's work is never done." But during those days, I found myself suffering with feelings of worthlessness. Feelings of insignificance. I thought to myself, "I am a college graduate. I should be doing something more significant than changing diapers, washing dishes, cleaning the house, preparing meals, and meeting my husband's needs." This was the mid-1970s and I was being inundated with messages from society that ratified my feelings of worthlessness and insignificance. Intentionally or unintentionally, the messages made me and other house-wives feel like nothing. I didn't know it at the time, but I was suffering power failure. I was not aware of my explosive inner power. Don't misunderstand me. I was not confused about my femininity (neither was my husband); I just did not know about my power as a woman. I did not know about the God-gift. I did not know how much influence I was capable of exerting in the home and in society. Can I share with you my powerful discovery?

We women were born with explosive inner power. We didn't earn it. We don't deserve it. It is a gift of God. We were created by God. "The Lord God formed man of the dust of the ground and breathed into his nostrils the breath of life, and man became a living being" (Genesis 2:7).

> And then God caused a deep sleep to fall on Adam, and he slept and He took one of his ribs and closed up the flesh in its place. Then the rib, which the Lord God had taken from man, He then made into a woman, and He brought her to the man. And Adam said, 'This is now bone of my bones and flesh of my flesh.' She shall be called Woman, because she was taken out of Man. (Genesis 2:21-23)

At Creation, the woman was endowed with so much power

that even Adam had to say, "Wooo–Man. Look at this creation!" We are extraordinary creations of God. Woman was the crowning act of His creation with power to procreate. That's power! Through the woman, God's command to be fruitful and multiply was fulfilled (Genesis 1:28). That's amazing power. Women were assigned distinctive duties more sacred, more holy, than those of man. As queen of her household, the woman "has in her power the molding of her children's characters."[1] God referenced the power of a woman in this way, "As is the mother, so is her daughter" (Ezekiel 16:44). The old worn but true statement says, "The hand that rocks the cradle rules the world." That sounds pretty powerful to me.

When I speak of power, I speak of influence, the ability to persuade through verbal and non-verbal force, and the ability to control outcomes by this unexplainable inner energy. Whether you know it or not, we women have a controlling influence much greater than we can imagine.

I was in a men's clothing store with my husband a while back and I had the best laugh. It was hilarious watching the men, including my husband, shop for clothes. They would march up to the suit rack with the confidence of a warrior and within minutes they would be looking around like little lambs for the woman or wife that came with them and timidly inquire, "Honey, do you like this one?" "No dear, that's not your style," the feminine fashion expert replied. For about an hour, I saw women exerting influence over the outcome of their man's clothing purchase. That's power!

The Bible is replete with examples of the controlling influence exerted by the explosive inner power of a woman for good or evil. Adam, the first man, was evicted from the Garden of Eden because of a woman (Genesis 3:6, 7); Samson, the strongest man who ever lived, was waylaid by a woman (Judges 16:4-20); Solomon, the wisest man in history, was made to look foolish because of women (1 Kings 11:1); David, the greatest king in Old Testament history, was lured into sin by the body of a beautiful woman (2 Samuel 11, 12); Miriam's wisdom led a nation (Exodus 15:20, 21); Esther's courage saved a nation (Esther 4:16); Dorcas served her community and the early church (Acts 9:36,39); and Rahab's faithfulness saved her family (Joshua 2:9-13).

Lest we become heady over this explosive inner power, we must remember, it is a gift. This power is your *being*. It is who you are as determined by God. We didn't earn it. We didn't purchase it. We don't even deserve it. God gifted us with this explosive inner power to use for the benefit of mankind and His glory. The challenge for women is recognizing this inner power, then using it wisely. Paul, writing to the Corinthian church, sought to address the struggle over the use of feminine power:

> Let your women keep silent in the churches; for they are not permitted to speak; but they are to be submissive, as the law also says. And if they want to learn something, let them ask their own husbands at home; for it is shameful for women to speak in church. (1 Corinthians 14:34, 35)

Paul was not seeking to strip women of their power, but simply to instruct them how, in that culture and during that time, to best exert their controlling influence. Paul was well aware of the power of women as portrayed in ancient times, in women such as Deborah, the judge and prophetess (Judges 4:4); Huldah and Anna, prophetesses (2 Kings 22:14; Luke 2:36); and the power of women as depicted by Solomon in his book of wisdom. Paul himself appreciated the influence of women as shown in inviting women to work alongside him in the gospel ministry (Philippians 4:3).

While in centuries past, women had been relegated to what appeared to be powerless positions, their influence was still felt. History makes it clear that position never determined the power of a woman. Her *being* determined her power. Just being a woman is power. Solomon, writing from revelation and experience, grappled with the inherent power of a woman.

And there a woman met him, with the attire of a harlot, and a crafty heart. She was loud and rebellious, her feet would not stay at home. At times she was outside, at times in the open square, lurking at every corner. So she caught him and kissed him; with an impudent face she said to him: 'I have peace offerings with me; Today I have paid my vows. So I came out to meet you, diligently to seek your face, and I have found you. I have spread my bed with tapestry. Colored coverings of Egyptian linen. I have perfumed my bed with myrrh, aloes, and cinnamon. Come, let us take our fill of love until morning; let us delight ourselves with love. For my husband is not at home; He has gone on a long journey; He has taken a bag of money with him, and will come home on the appointed day.' With her enticing speech she caused him to yield, with her flattering lips she seduced him. Immediately he went after her, as an ox goes to the slaughter, or as a fool to the cor-

rection of the stocks. Till an arrow struck his liver.
As a bird hastens to the snare, he did not know
it would cost his life. (Proverbs 7:10-23)

What would cause a man to sacrifice everything, including his life? Only a woman. Almost half of the 31 chapters in Proverbs refer to this explosive inner power of a woman, mostly in negative ways. Yet, Solomon obviously held women in high regard. He personifies Wisdom as a woman and he ends the wisdom literature by describing the virtuous woman. Solomon captures the power of a woman in these final words, "Who can find a virtuous wife? For her worth is far above rubies" (Proverbs 31:10).

This power found in women is an inner dynamo. It is divine effulgence – a brilliant radiance. It is a feminine electromagnet that has nothing to do with looks, gifts, age, or place of birth. It is a mystery too deep to explain but too apparent to dismiss.

My Secret Weapon

This power found in women is an inner dynamo. It is divine effulgence – a brilliant radiance. It is a feminine electro-magnet that has nothing to do with looks, gifts, age, or place of birth. It is a mystery too deep to explain but too apparent to dismiss."

– Dr. Susie M. Hill

My Secret Weapon

Chapter Two
The Power Surge

"It takes a woman." That's a statement I often repeat to my husband. Although said in jest, I have observed that the feminine perspective provides an important lens within the construct of marriage, family, and society. But often our perspectives and influence are not heard or felt until a power surge. I use the term power surge to describe the sudden burst of feminine power exerted in the home, church, and society. Women have always played a significant role in the outcome of society, but many major contributions made by women were the result of power surges. You know what I mean. Our lot has been like the poor man in Ecclesiastes: "Nevertheless the poor man's wisdom is despised, and his words are not heard" (Ecclesiastes 9:16). We are not heard until the house is burning down. Our power isn't tapped into until the lights are out. You see, our power can't be denied, so often it is intentionally overlooked while searching for answers and power in other places. Then, finally, when all else has failed, we women are sought out for answers and influence. This happens with my husband and me. After my wise counsel (okay, my opinion) and his failed attempts, he finally decides to listen, and then he says, "I know now why I married you." Now don't misunderstand me; as women, we are not always right. Nor are all our insights and inputs correct. What I am saying is that the feminine perspective is indeed as needful as the masculine perspective and sometimes more powerful. It is a perspective that emanates from our inner being. It transcends outer beauty. It's the inner core of a woman. The Bible mentions specifically that some women, such as Eve, Sarah, Rebekah, and Esther, were fair to look upon, while others such as Rahab and Ruth had no mention of their outward appearance. Yet each had enormous impact, especially during a power surge. They experienced what many of us have experienced – deep insights that come from a place we do not even understand ourselves that often result in a power surge that saves the day.

Abigail had one of those power surges after her drunken husband, Nabal, arrogantly refused to fulfill a simple request for food from the fugitive future king of Israel, David. David saw Nabal's refusal as disrespectful and undeserving. He had been kind to Nabal's herdsmen. For months, David and his men had provided armed protection for Nabal's grazing flocks. Common courtesy warranted kind treatment of David and his men. Enraged, David stormed off determined to kill Nabal and all his male servants.

Abigail's influence at home was evidenced in the servants' reporting of Nabal's foolish, arrogant, and selfish behavior. Once she heard the evil report, Abigail understood that a power surge was needed. Abigail mounted her donkey, rushed to David, and activated her explosive feminine power, which surged and defused David's anger, saving the lives of her servants and ultimately winning his favor (1 Samuel 25:23-35).

Again, this explosive inner power of a woman transcends skin tone, hair color, shape, or the size of a woman. It is an inner force so powerful that it must be covered with humility and dressed in modest apparel. Feminine power surges are proof positive of the explosive inner power of a woman. That is why I am so passionate about teaching women how to use this power responsibly. Feminine power is not a toy. It is not some low-voltage power. This mysterious inner energy is high-voltage power with the potential to destroy. Truth be told, most women don't recognize this awesome power. We don't believe we have power like that of Queen Esther.

Queen Esther is a primary example of one of the most powerful women in biblical history. Esther lived during a very critical period of Jewish history. It was during the time when Israel lay on the garbage heap of history. The chosen people of God were in a hostile land, ruled over by a people of great cruelty. Satan had planned to annihilate the Jews through Haman, the Secretary of State to King Ahasuerus of Persia, but God had in place a woman. Again, while I place a high value on men, I do believe that sometimes, "It takes a woman." After Queen Vashti's unfortunate dismissal, King Ahasuerus began a search to replace the deposed queen. The scripture records that his search ended with a young Jewish girl. "He loved Esther more than all the other women, and she obtained grace and favor in his sight more than all the virgins, so he set the royal crown upon her head and made her queen instead of Vashti" (Esther 2:17). Why do you suppose Esther found favor with the king above all the other women? I believe it was because of her modesty more than her outer beauty. Esther was a product of the Jewish community that intentionally taught modesty to women. As a Jewish woman, Esther practiced Tzniut (Tzni-oot).[1] Tzniut are laws concerned with modesty as reflected in both dress and behavior. It is used to describe both character traits of modesty and humility. For the Jews, Tzniut was not mere law but

a way of life. Esther, like all orthodox Jewish women, lived
by Tzniut at home and abroad. It was the management of
her explosive inner power through modesty that won her the
favor of the king. Later, that same feminine inner dynamo
surged after her uncle Mordecai informed her of the sinister
plot to annihilate the Jewish people. Her feminine power
was activated at its highest level. Queen Esther, cloaked in
humility and dressed in modest apparel, with the intuition
and a plan that only a woman can have, went before the
king. Esther understood what I want all women to understand; few men can resist the power surge of an intelligent,
beautiful woman. King Ahasuerus' position was no match
for Queen Esther's explosive inner power. Esther's responsible use of her feminine power saved her life and the lives
of the Jewish people. Women, don't you see, we have power.
We don't need to fight for it. We were born with power. We
didn't earn it. We didn't purchase it. It is a God-gift. Our
challenge, women, is learning how to harness and manage
this God-gift properly.

My Secret Weapon

"This explosive inner power of women transcends skin tone, hair color, shape, or the size of a woman. It is an inner force so powerful that it must be covered with humility and dressed in modest apparel."

– Dr. Susie M. Hill

Chapter Three
Modesty - Managing the Power

I am not the fix-it type woman. I am the traditional female who loves to see my man get sweaty in the yard while I give detailed instructions on what to do. I love to see him take the lead in managing the repairs around the house. By the way, my husband is like Bill Cosby when it comes to home repairs; when he puts on his tool belt, be prepared to call the plumber or the carpenter. In a discussion some time ago with my husband, he shared with me the difference between 110/120 voltage and 220/240 voltage. The 110/120 voltage is used to power small to medium-size appliances, he instructed. He continued, "large appliances, like stoves and clothes dryers, require the higher 220/240 voltage." I saw this as an excellent analogy to describe the difference between the power of men and the power of women. Men are wired with 110/120 voltage. Great power. Important current. In fact, here in America, most appliances operate on 110/120 voltage. But there are some things that require higher voltage. Some situations and circumstances demand greater power, and we women are wired to handle them. We operate on 220/240 voltage. Maybe that's why we are so emotional. Could this also answer the question of hot flashes? Remember, "It takes a woman." Now please don't push the analogy too hard. I am by no means attempting to make us women into a class of superheroines, even though at times we act like we are. I'm just emphasizing the magnitude of the power. "For everyone to whom much is given, from him much will be required; and to whom much has been committed, of him they will ask the more" (Luke 12:48). We have been entrusted with 220/240 power; therefore, it is critical that we learn how to harness and manage it. Mismanaged 110/120 voltage shocks. Mismanaged 220/240 voltage kills.

God does require proper management of our explosive inner power. We discover in the parable of the talents that management is mandatory (Matthew 25:14-30). Each servant in the parable was required by the master to invest his/her talent wisely and responsibly. The servants who saw the power and potential of their talents and invested them wisely were blessed and honored by God. But one servant devalued his gift, hid his one talent, and refused to invest his gift. He was condemned and judged by God. He was cast into utter darkness (Matthew 25:30). As a woman of God, you are given responsibility for the appropriate use of your power. And just like the servants in the parable, God will hold you accountable for its use or misuse.

After more than thirty years as a mother, mentor, and seminar presenter, I have found that the greatest challenge for women is the awareness of this God-given power, along with how to harness and manage it responsibly. My observations uncovered three groups of women that surface in the discussion of managing feminine power. The first group is comprised of the women who are well aware of their power and have learned from mothers or others how to use their power responsibly. In the second group are the women who are almost totally oblivious of their God-gift. And because of their lack of awareness, they never tap into their power for their personal good or the good of others. Finally, there is the group of women who are keenly aware of their explosive inner power but use it for sinister purposes, wreaking havoc on the world as did evil Queen Jezebel. I believe that most women fall into the second group of women. I believe that many wonderful women, God-fearing women, just do not know that they have this explosive inner power. Many women are in search of power they already have. It bears repeating – we were born with power. We didn't earn it. We didn't purchase it. It's a God-gift. Our challenge, women, is becoming aware of this power and then learning how to harness and manage this God-gift responsibly.

How do we properly manage our feminine power? The Bible is clear: "Whether you eat or drink, or whatever you do, do all to the glory of God" (1 Corinthians 10:31). We are to exemplify the image of the Creator and magnify His name through the proper use of this power. The overarching principle for managing our feminine power in Paul's admonition to Timothy, his son in the ministry, was "In like manner also, that women adorn themselves in modest apparel, with propriety and moderation, not with braided hair or gold or pearls or costly clothing, but, which is proper for women professing godliness, with good works" (1 Timothy 2:9, 10). Modesty is the principle for managing our explosive inner power.

I am well-aware that *modesty* is a loaded word that carries negative baggage and can turn some women off. But please don't hit the switch. Let me explain. After years of agonizing with the word modesty myself, I assure you I will not use modesty to measure hemlines, necklines, or religious lines. Sadly and regrettably, the discussion of modesty has been almost exclusively focused on the external. It's been only about a cover-up. Let me repeat again to my sisters, I am now more keenly aware than ever of the role of dress in expressing our femininity and will, in this book, share with you my discovery about dress. But this is not a book about dress. This is a book about *being*. It is about the awareness of who we are as women. It is about reaffirming that we are extraordinary creations of God with explosive inner power. I use the word modesty in this book to inspire, motivate, and empower you. As the voice for feminine responsible living, I am committed to teaching you how to masterfully use your weapon. I have moved the discussion of modesty from the external to the internal, from clothes to character, from dress to destiny. So journey with me as we look at the dimensions of modesty that unlock your explosive inner power.

My Secret Weapon

"When it comes to 'saving the world,'
or part of it, street by street, neighborhood
by neighborhood, women are the catalysts
through whom the critical mass for social
change will be achieved."

– Patricia Aburdene and John Naisbitt

My Secret Weapon

Chapter Four
The Dimensions of Modesty

It happened in the 8th grade at San Diego Academy, the private Christian school my mother worked sacrificially to afford so that my siblings and I could attend. I was working as a student helper at the school library in my new blue long-sleeve polyester dress. It was the late 1960s and the new hot fashion fabric was polyester. You remember polyester, don't you? It was that soft, silky, shiny material that I thought looked good. As I went to ask the male head librarian a question, the buttons that went down the entire length of my dress popped completely opened. I was embarrassed. My only response was to do an immediate about-face and as inconspicuously as possible re-button my dress. Modesty required me to quickly cover up. The word modesty simply means to cover up. I found myself naturally wanting to cover myself. So as I have grown as a woman, in my search to understand the meaning of covering up, the topic of modesty has been of great interest.

I am not a biblical scholar, but I am a student of God's Word. I tease my husband, the preacher, from time to time with this statement, "I'm not a preacher, but I sure know a good sermon when I hear one." Likewise, I am not a theologian, but I know Bible truth when I read it. My discussion in this chapter, then, is not an exegesis (a scholarly critical examination) of Paul's passage on modesty. Rather, I present findings from my personal study, meditation, and years of struggling to understand what Paul meant in the famous text used often to whip women into line in regard to modesty.

What I have uncovered, I believe, is the core of Paul's meaning about modesty. To me it is obvious: Paul's major concern was for the inner development of a woman. Unlike the culture and church of his day, which had a one-dimensional focus on the external – the cover-up, Paul wrote about the three dimensions of modesty: cultivating the power, covering the power, and dressing the power. "And I want women to get in there with men in humility before God, not primping before a mirror or chasing the latest fashion but doing something beautiful for God and becoming beautiful doing it" (1 Timothy 2:9, The Message). There it is. Modesty for Paul was the *being*, not the *doing*. Understanding Paul's view allows the discussion of modesty to be broader and deeper. It allows the discussion to be about the awareness of who we are as women and reaffirm that we are extraordinary creations of God with explosive inner power. It allows us to see modesty as the method of managing our feminine power instead of using it as a tool for censorship. As mentioned earlier, our feminine mystique is so powerful, it must be covered with humility and dressed in modest apparel. Covering up is really about managing the power. Let's look at the three dimensions of modesty: Cultivating the Power, Covering the Power, and Dressing Up the Power.

Cultivating the Power

The first dimension of modesty is cultivating the power. Yes, we are born with this explosive inner power, but it is raw, undeveloped power. It is power without restraints, and left to itself and uncultivated, will do untold damage as it self-destructs. To become a responsible woman, the core of our *being* must be developed. Our womanhood has to be cultivated. The explosive inner power must be tamed. This is not a task that we do alone. There are no self-made women. Our feminine power is molded and shaped in the context of community.

The older women likewise, that they be reverent in behavior, not slanderers, not given to much wine, teachers of good things – that they admonish the young women to love their husbands, to love their children, to be discreet, chaste, homemakers, good, obedient to their own husbands, that the word of God may not be blasphemed. (Titus 2:3-5)

Modesty implies living life in the community because community is the place where modesty is cultivated. When I think of my own development as a woman, I know without a doubt that I would not be the woman I am without community. My community started with my home church. There, I was exposed to women of all social standings. There were the working-class women, like my own mother, who fought to keep their families together but never fudged on their femininity. They helped me cultivate my inner strength as a woman. There were the professional women along with my mother, who encouraged me to pursue higher education. My community expanded when I left home as a teenager to attend college where I found female Christian professors and young ladies who inspired and taught me how to use my explosive inner power responsibly. In ministry as a young bride, I thank God for women like Etta Dudley, the wife of our first conference president, who modeled team ministry; Dorothy Beets, an instructor in the class *Fascinating Woman-hood*, taught me that I held the key to the happiness in my home; and Lucille Hill, my mother-in-law, who labored beside her husband in ministry for over 60 years, cultivated in me the wisdom of being a wife and mother. Then there was Suzette Trousdale, a member of one our former churches. She would have been the most unlikely candidate to help cultivate the explosive inner power of any woman, let alone me. Ms. Trousdale was neglected at a young age, misunderstood by family and community, married several times, and strong and feisty enough to fight any man or woman. Having a tongue so sharp, witty, and potent, few people dared tangle with her. But at her core, Ms. Trousdale was a woman who knew her explosive inner power, which she learned from a hard life and real world experience. At a New Year's Eve service one year, Ms. Trousdale stood up and announced one of her New Year's resolutions. "I will get married this year," she spoke with the confidence of a young woman, even though she was in her mid-fifties. Just as she was about to sit down, Ms. Trousdale heard a few cynical mumbles. She turned, and with wit and boldness blurted out, "It will happen. I have five men to choose from." A few months later, my husband officiated at the wedding ceremony in which she married one of the five men. She was happily married and deeply in love with him until the day he died. It was Ms. Trousdale, the epitome of womanhood in dress and grace, who stopped me one day and said, "Young lady, a woman isn't fully dressed until she is wearing a hat and gloves and carrying a handbag." Shortly afterward, I went out and bought my first of many hats. I will tell you, I started feeling like a woman. Doors literally started opening for me, as men found themselves unconsciously responding to my femininity. Modesty is shaped in community.

My friend, Myrtle Glascoe, a single parent, understood the power of community as a means of cultivating the inner power of a woman. A few years ago, Myrtle invited my husband and me to her daughter Mariama's wedding. Having been Mariama's principal in the fourth grade, I was not surprised that the invitation ended with an emphatic statement, "You will be at Mariama's wedding." My husband and I were considered family; therefore, missing the wedding wasn't an option. Not until I arrived did I fully understand her insistence of my presence at this milestone event for her only daughter. In a tender conversation the day after the wedding, Myrtle confided in me that she had not raised her daughter alone. With tears in her eyes, she spoke of the five women God sent into her life at crucial periods to help parent her daughter. She described her daily routine as a graduate student, then university professor, that would have been impossible to manage without the help of women who said, "Let me help you with Mariama, while you go and do what you must do." All five women, considered by Myrtle to be Mariama's other mothers, came to celebrate. The morning before the wedding, in a special, intimate ritual adopted from an African tradition, these adopted mothers surrounded Mariama and "poured words of wisdom into her" as she prepared for the institution of marriage. I understood then why Myrtle wanted me there. I was considered one of Mariama's community mothers. "It takes a village to raise a child." And it takes a community to cultivate the power of a woman.

Covering the Power

Covering the power is the second dimension of modesty. From my observation, many women are encouraged to dress up the power before they cover up the power. But the feminine power is so awesome, it must first be covered with the undergarment of humility. I believe that was Paul's major concern in his instruction on modesty. Humility is a woman's spiritual covering. It is her spiritual undergarment woven in the gifts of the Spirit. "Clothe yourselves with humility toward one another, because God opposes the proud but gives grace to the humble" (1 Peter 5:5 NIV). Humility is learning how to walk in humble service before God and man.

It was Ruth's humility that won the heart of Boaz when he discovered the devotion Ruth had for her mother-in-law.

> Entreat me not to leave you, or to turn back from following after you; for wherever you go, I will go, and wherever you lodge, I will lodge. Your people shall be my people, and your God my God. Where you die, I will die, and there will I be buried. The Lord do so to me, and more also, if anything but death parts you and me. (Ruth 1:16,17)

Humility is not a natural feminine attribute. It is a gift from God that comes in a life submitted to Christ. I have found that in order to keep my undergarment of humility on and fresh, I must practice the spiritual disciplines of prayer, fasting, Bible study, meditation, worship, and service daily. The explosive inner power of a woman is extremely potent – left uncovered it is dangerous. It bears repeating in still another way: your feminine power exposed is like uninsulated electric wire plugged into a 220/240 power source. Don't do it. Cover your explosive inner power with humility. And when you cultivate and cover your inner power, you will discover, as I have, that you become irresistible.

Dressing up the Power

The third and final dimension of modesty is dressing up the power. Much has been written about how Christian women should dress. And much of what is written is focused on hemlines, necklines, and religious lines. In any discussion of modesty, what a woman wears cannot be overlooked. It's the elephant in the room that you can't get around but the elephant in the room that is extremely explosive. I know from personal experience how explosive it is to deal with this topic of dressing up the power. I have reached out to young women in the past about covering up, only to leave singed and reluctant to approach women on the topic. But know this, in chapters Seven and Eight where I cover this dimension in more detail, I promise that my perspective will be fresh, deep, different, and enjoyable. I encourage you to keep reading.

"Numerous studies have shown that the surge in pants wear corresponded to the more or less conscious desire on the part of most women to affirm their equality with men by dressing like them."

— Francois Boucher and Yvonne Deslanders

My Secret Weapon

Chapter Five

Modesty – It Is What It Is

In the first four chapters, I intentionally spent time laying the spiritual foundation. I have discovered that a solid foundation is crucial for surviving the storms in life and the discussions in life. This is especially true with the topic of modesty. The topic of modesty often gets stuck in the mud because we just haven't spent the time digging deep to lay the foundation. We've spent much of the time on the surface with the *doing* of modesty and very little time laying the foundation with the *being* of modesty. Therefore, the topic of modesty is avoided, ignored, or disregarded. Since a solid foundation has been laid, we can now frame the topic.

Have you heard the expression, "It is what it is," or for my Spanish-speaking sisters, "Es lo que es"? The expression simply means, *take what you see or experience at face value.* Don't spend time seeking to understand the reason why or

the reason how; just see it for what it is. That's what I do
in this chapter. I build on the foundation of modesty the
framework of social theory that "attempts to discuss and explain what is, not what it should be."[1] Social theory is the "It
is what it is" of social science research. Social science research
is done with the idea of gaining a better understanding of
the phenomenon by getting as close as possible to the phenomenon. It does not purport to give solutions or solve any
concerns surrounding a social issue. It just reports its finding. So why conduct research? Good question. Research allows us to ask questions or simply make observations, giving
us an opportunity to better understand what we face in daily
life. It gives us a better understanding of what is. It allows us
to make sense about the things that we observe from which
we are able to develop theories. When I use the word *theory*,
it means "to look at, view, or contemplate." Theories are just
scientific observations. They are not, however, rulebooks.
Theories were not designed as guides to order one's life. Nor
are they principles that lead to success and happiness. For
example, the feminist theory is a philosophical, political perspective that focuses on how gender and power have shaped
our patriarchal society. In studying the theory, we discover
that the main goal of feminism is to shed light on women's
experiences in hopes of creating an equal society for all hu-

man beings.[2] It simply looks at how women were viewed in society but does not solve the issues of women in society. However, looking at the way women were viewed in society helped us to see that change was and is needed. While the research itself didn't bring about change, it has resulted in the awareness of and possible solutions to some women's issues as feminine researchers used their findings to become crusaders on behalf of women.

For the purposes of this discussion on the explosive inner power of a woman, I will apply two theoretical perspectives: phenomenology and gestalt theory, as a way of building a framework to gain a better understanding of the feminine power.

Phenomenology

Phenomenology is a theoretical perspective that states that people make sense of their lives by giving meaning to it.[3] I have chosen the phenomenological approach to better understand the role fashion and dress play in the demonstration of a woman's power. In the book *Megatrends for Women*, we find that what a woman chooses to wear allows her to exert, use, and demonstrate her explosive inner power. Although some women may consider buying clothes as a leisure activity, it is the place where a woman exercises her power, her *being*.[4]

Richard Alapack, an associate professor of psychology in his excellent research using phenomenology, unravels the historical significance of the culture of fashion and the role of the fashion industry in determining which body regions to reveal or conceal. His observations are critical to explaining how designers have manipulated the explosive inner power of women through fashion. He states, "Each passing fad, as it lingers and fades, pinpoints the crux of its historical moment and thus bears theoretical significance."[5] In other words, throughout history, fashion communicates loudly what is transpiring in society. For example, during the Victorian era, about the 19th century, there was a change in the male and female dress, which reflected the changing ideals of beauty. The dresses worn during this period showed subtle feminine displays of a woman. It was considered flirtatious for a woman to swing her crinoline (a stiffened petticoat) in such a way that allowed a tantalizing glimpse of her ankle.

In her article entitled, *Looking Good: College Women and Body Image, 1875-1930*, Margaret Lowe examined the meanings that Smith College women gave to the fashions that were popular during the 1920s. She saw how the female students "shaped their….attitudes about looks and self-presentations, with dating and marriage very much in mind."[6] Lowe saw how these college women linked fashion to women's progress. She observed the changing ideas about femininity and feminism, managing changing ideas of both as well as their role in a national consumer culture.[7] These women from Smith College saw fashion as being functional, modest, and in good taste. They questioned the tradition that required the female students to wear a cumbersome medieval cap and gown to class. This proved to be impractical, and was especially evident during warm weather. The Smith College women also protested the rule that required knickers (short, knee-length trousers sometimes called "bloomers") to be worn only during sports activities and not on public transportation or main streets. It was difficult trying to ride a bicycle with the long skirts while wearing knickers. The women indicated that the knickers were neat and much more convenient to wear as they rode their bicycles.[8] Lowe's research with the Smith College women illustrates that women reflect their values through their dress.

Gestalt Theory

The word *gestalt* is a German word that roughly translates as "whole" or "form." Gestalt theory focuses on how the mind perceives and processes information.[9] Although gestalt theory relates to disciplines including art, music, psychology, and instructional design, the theory can also allow us to see the shifts that take place in human experiences. For the purposes of this discussion, I will consider the gestalt shifts that have occurred in fashion and the interplay between these shifts and the captivating power of a woman.

Gestalt shifts have occurred throughout history regarding appropriate dress for women. A gestalt shift was observed among women during the social unrest of the 1960s. Many women went bra-less as a sign of taking control of their freedom and independence. Then in 1984, fashion designers Jean-Paul Gaultier, Vivienne Westwood, and Azzedine Alaia decided to promote the concept of underwear-as-outerwear.[10] It was during this shift that pop music star Madonna made it fashionable to wear undergarments as outergarments. That fashion became mainstream in 2001. These shifts were never accidental, but instead emerged with intentionality. As Alapack describes,

> radical modes of dress first emerged on the runway, and at 'gala events' which showcased pop stars, actors, and musicians. Eventually, a raging popular fad emerged that exposed the stomach,

belly button, and the lowest part of a woman's back (interpretation). Various labels designate this trend, the bare-bellybutton look, the lowest part of a woman's back-cracked chic, the visible G-string syndrome, the assets-flashed (interpretation), the open waistband look, and the visible underwear style. Each of these interchangeable labels depicts one aspect of an identifiable gestalt: the epiphany (or showing) of flesh and skin.[11]

In New York, The Museum at FIT collects, conserves, documents, and interprets fashion. It is a think tank for fashion studies. It is an ambitious program of scholarly publications, new initiatives, and research application for student scholars and designers. The Museum at FIT surveyed 250 years of feminine allurement in fashion in the presentation of "Seduction." Through the prism of fashion, a visual history is given of the relationship between seduction and clothing; feminine allurement; moral standards; and social norms. According to The Museum at FIT, "By the 1980s and 1990s, attitudes towards the display of women's bodies had shifted dramatically, and female allure was increasingly considered as a sign of strength. Today, contemporary fashion has shifted again. The focus in fashion now is on beautiful fabrics and on sensuousness rather than on exposure of skin."[12] Now we can understand better why it is very common to see body-revealing and form-fitting romantic styles prevailing in today's women's fashions.

Gestalt theory also deals with three concepts that demonstrate the relationship between visual perception and the whole of a composition. The three concepts are awareness, closure, and continuation. I apply them to illustrate the dynamics of dress on the explosive inner power of a woman.

Awareness

Awareness is one of the primary components of gestalt theory. It is being in touch with your own experience while making contact with the world around you. Awareness involves keeping an open mind and being genuinely curious to find out how we go about being who we are, at every level of our being.[13] When considering the awareness of women in regard to their secret weapon, I believe that a lot of women just fall in line and unquestioningly accept current fashions. It appears that some women are oblivious to the messages being communicated through their clothing or they just don't know that what they are wearing does have an impact. Advertisers know and are very aware of the feminine power.

They understand that their sales will increase by as much as 30 percent just by putting a picture of a woman on the cover.[14] This increase in sales occurs regardless of the product being sold. It bears repeating, advertisers understand the feminine power and use the power of a woman to boost their sales. Please don't miss this: the increase in sales has nothing to do with what is being sold, it is the captivating force of a woman that pulls the buyer in. While advertisers know this, there are many women who are still unaware of their captivating power. They don't understand who they are or that they even possess such power.

I believe that the women from Smith College demonstrated their awareness of who they were and the message they wanted to communicate about themselves through fashion. It was in 1920, after the historical movement that gave women the right to vote, that the women from this small college began a "dress reform movement." These college women wanted to bring fashion back to what they understood as an appropriate form of self-presentation. They saw the current fashions of their time as controversial. For them, there was no conflict between modesty and beauty. They believed that women could dress in appropriate clothing without forfeiting good taste.

One of the fashion changes that occurred with women

during this time was cutting the hair into the bob, a short chin-length hairstyle that became very popular in the 1920s. This cut was celebrated as a crowning achievement for women's equality.[15] Although the short length was more difficult to maintain than the longer-length hair, the college women saw the short chin-length haircut as a form of emancipation from the traditions that kept women bound. The haircut permitted them to express their femininity, not just through their dress but also in their hairstyles.

The dress reform movement at Smith College posed some concerns about gender and feminine power. Some women took advantage of the new opportunities that women were given in the 1920s to assert themselves through their clothing and appearance. Therefore, some of the new fashions, while negotiating social acceptance among some, became a symbol of feminine assertiveness to others. Fashion served as an arena in which the students could explore and manage the changing ideas about feminine power.[16] However, the Smith College women used fashion to express their feminine power in ways that made it possible for them to experience social success and improve their identity.

Designers are aware that dress is perhaps the most significant way a woman demonstrates the use of her power. They know that women, by and large, wear whatever clothing is in style. Every woman wants to look good every time she steps outside of her home. That's a good thing. But we need to also know that everything a woman wears sends a message.[17] Again, I repeat, designers know this all so well. It appears that the designers have a deeper understanding of the explosive inner power of a woman through her dress than does the woman herself. Designers seem to understand that "the human body is not only an object of observation, but also a meaning-creating subject and a medium of culture."[18]

During each significant segment of history, fashion designers have singled out some section of the female skin as sensuous. This, of course, is not something that the fashion industry has done openly. However, despite the disclaimers from the fashion industry, and other venues, such as advertising, entertainment, cosmetics, diet, fitness, and tanning, the incessant massive exploitation of women remains ingrained in the culture of our society.[19]

Closure

The concept of closure illustrates the idea that "grouping" items together tends to complete the entity. A complex object that is seen with your eyes is a collection of simple items that your mind puts together as a single entity. For example, a face is a collection of eyes, ears, nose, mouth, and so forth. You can recognize a familiar face, even if part of the face is hidden from you. If you put a hat or sunglasses on the face, your mind supplies the missing parts of the face if enough of the significant features are visible. An example of this aspect of the gestalt theory can also be illustrated with the series of circles as shown in Figure 1. The circle remains evident to you, even when segments of it are removed. Thus, the concept of closure depicts what happens with the missing identifiable pieces; the mind closes the image by supplying the missing parts.[20]

Figure 1

This concept of closure does not just work with geometric shapes. It can also be used to explain what happens with the explosive inner power of a woman. A research study was conducted to see the response of men seated in a room when a provocatively dressed woman entered. The results showed that in every occurrence, the men looked at the woman.[21]

This happened without regard to the age of the man, or even his profession. That is just the way it is. "It is what it is," women. So when a woman wears a top that reveals only her bellybutton she is sadly mistaken to believe that only her belly button is revealed. The mind supplies the missing pieces. The peek-a-boo into her belly button does not stop there. Closure says that the mind will supply the missing pieces of the composition. That's just the way it is. "It is what it is," women.

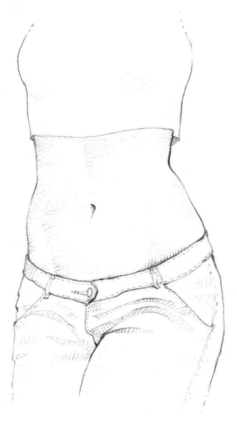

Continuation

The concept of continuation describes what happens
when the viewer's attention is drawn to a composition. It
is based on the premise that once the eyes start looking
in a particular direction they will continue in that direction until they see something significant.[22] I was sitting on
the second row in a worship service of a church during the
week of spiritual revival called "Jam 94" where my husband
and I were presenters. During the week, I noticed that the
women dressed in the finest apparel. They did not wear
ordinary clothes to church. They were dressed in two-piece
suits or beautiful dresses. I noted an absence of short, tight,
or revealing clothing of any sort, and the women looked
fabulous. On the last day of the revival, just after the worship service started, a young woman, who appeared to be in
her early 20s came in and sat next to me. She was wearing a
beautiful two-piece off-white suit with a long skirt. Before
I knew it, just after she sat down and crossed her legs, the
bishop's wife, who was seated on my left, took a large scarf
and draped it over the young woman's legs to cover the split
in her skirt that gave everyone a view "all the way to China."
When she walked down the aisle, she provided a full view of

her legs under the apron-like skirt. You see, when a woman wears a skirt that has a split in it, according to the concept of continuation, once the eyes of a man start looking in a particular direction, (say the split starts at the bottom), his eyes will continue until his eyes land on something significant. In this young woman's case, it would be "China."

The argument for modesty is justified and now framed even by social theory. We can debate, deny, or disregard it, but "It is what it is."

My Secret Weapon

"Fashion involves more than simply imitating another person's style. It is a form of nonverbal communication that provides a way for people to express their identities and values."

– The World Book Encyclopedia

My Secret Weapon

Chapter Six
The Weapon

There you have it. Women have explosive inner power. We didn't earn it. We didn't purchase it. We don't even deserve it. It is our birthright as daughters of God. It is a God-gift that can't be destroyed or denied. This explosive inner power of women, with its alluring cover, has been certified by biblical foundations and ratified by the framework of social theory in the earlier chapters. In the following chapters it will be actualized. What I mean by actualized is how the power is used. "Inner power" has been used to describe the mystery of the feminine power, but when I speak of the use of this power, I call it "my weapon."

A weapon is an instrument designed to inflict injury or death to an opponent or to defend, protect, or rescue an individual, friend, or companion. It is an instrument that can be used for good or evil. Initially, I wanted to title this book *My Secret Weapon: Unlocking the Power of Modesty in a Woman*. I was advised that the use of the word modesty might turn some women away. It is as charged as the weapon that I am unlocking in this book. Why is that? Well, perhaps it dates back to the period of the Reformation when Gnosticism, a Greek philosophy, penetrated the early church's teaching which asserts that the material world, including the body, is evil and the spiritual world is good.[1] If a person wanted to experience the highest level of spirituality, then they had to deny themselves anything that related to the material world. Since the body is material, according to the Gnostics, it should be covered up and considered an evil that should be kept under extreme subjection. Therefore, the inner power of a woman, covered in an alluring body, was considered dangerous and potentially evil. It was this erroneous philosophy that distorted the discussion of the feminine power and that has contributed to the negative views of modesty. It was said by Henry Chadwick in *The Early Church* that, "The conquest of Gnosticism may be counted the hardest and most decisive battle in church history."[2]

Your explosive inner power and its alluring covering are not evil, just powerful. It is a weapon that can be used for good or evil. There's a charming story about a successful CEO who was traveling with his wife along an interstate highway when he noticed that the car was low on gas. He got off the highway at the next exit and soon found a run-down, one-pump gas station. The CEO asked the attendant to fill the tank and check the oil, and then went for a little walk to stretch his legs.

As he returned to the car, the husband noticed that the attendant and his wife were engaged in an animated conversation. The conversation stopped as the CEO paid the attendant. But as he was getting back into the car, he noticed the attendant wave and heard him say, "It was great talking to you again." When they drove off, the CEO asked his wife if she knew that man. She said, "Yes, in fact we went to high school together and dated steadily for about a year."

"Boy, were you lucky that I came along," bragged the husband. "If you had married him, you'd be the wife of a gas station attendant instead of the wife of a successful chief executive officer."

"Oh honey," replied the wife, "if I had married him, he'd be the chief executive officer and you'd be the gas station attendant."[3]

While this story is a witty illustration of a woman's power, it demonstrates that how we use our explosive inner power, our weapon, can make or break not only men, but children, communities, and society. What I discovered is that while we have been victimized as women, we should never see ourselves as victims. In spite of male chauvinism, centuries of abuse, and millennia of walking and working in the shadows of men, we still have power. In 2010, it is estimated that women control nearly 60 percent of the wealth in America.[4] That's power. According to a recent survey, the typical congregation in the United States is 61% female.[5] That's a lot of power. One hundred percent of all natural births in the world are by women. That's world-controlling power. We determine to a large extent how the world goes. We are not victims. We just aren't aware of our explosive inner power; hence, we don't know how to use our weapon. Think about it. Men spend their lives trying to please a woman: a mother, grandmother, girlfriend, wife, sister, or some female in their lives. Jonathan Slocumb, the Christian comedian, performs a scene of a tough young man from the hood being arrested. As he is being marched off to the police car handcuffed, he notices the television cameramen taping him. With tears coming down his cheeks, he shouts into the camera, "Tell my Mamma I said hey."

Don't misunderstand me, women have power, but we do not have all power. Only God has all power. And while women have enormous power, men also have power and position that we must honor and respect. And we honor and respect their power and position by the way we use our weapon.

Women do carry a powerful weapon, so it is imperative that we use it responsibly. This feminine weapon is made of three components: maternal attraction, a sixth sense, and allurement. The maternal attraction is influence that results from birthing the world. Motherhood has inherent power; Jonathan Slocumb's comedic scene attests to that fact. Mothers can often break through when no one else can. Then there is the sixth sense. It's that God-given intuition that defies reasoning. We women will often say, "I just sense something is wrong." How do you know? "I don't know," we reply, "I just have that feeling." The feminine sixth sense has saved many lives and safeguarded many relationships. And finally, there is the allurement. There is something about the covering of a woman that is tantalizing and often mesmerizing. The curves, the skin, and the hair combine to form a magnetic force. Whether we are tall or short, thin or thick, dark or light, have short hair or long hair, the allure is there. A woman's body is attractive and desirable. King David experienced the power of feminine allurement. "Then it happened one evening that David arose from his bed and walked on the roof of the king's house. And from the roof he saw a woman bathing, and the woman was very beautiful to behold" (2 Samuel 11:2). I hope you get the picture. These three components combined create a feminine mystique that is a powerful weapon.

Your inner being covered in feminine allurement is your explosive inner power that then becomes your weapon. And since your explosive inner power never shuts down, your weapon is always activated. Consequently, as women, we must always be alert to how we are using our weapon. Whether we know it or not, our weapon is being used for good or evil. It is being used for self-glory or God's glory. It is being used to hurt or to heal. We determine the outcome.

Joan of Arc is one of the most remarkable people to ever live. Her name is easily recognized by virtually everyone in the world today. Joan's life and history are also among the best documented of anyone who has ever lived outside of modern times; however, most people are not aware of all that this simple young woman from a small town in eastern France accomplished in her life and death. Joan saved her people and united all of France by winning several important battles at Orleans and Patay in what is now known as the Hundred Years War. Joan completely reversed the course of this war and kept France from becoming a colony of the English. Greatly celebrated by her own people, she was hated by the English, who ultimately captured her and rigged a trial under the auspices of the church to justify burning her at the stake. Twenty-five years later, the illegality of her trial was revealed in another trial held by the church that completely exonerated her and declared her a martyr. She remains one of the most beloved figures in all of history. Many believe that it was her feminine power, used as a weapon, that saved a nation.[6]

"Since American women won the vote, their victorious ranks have separated into two camps; one portion is demanding an even greater measure of equality; the other is beginning to wonder which is more desirable, equality or chivalry, and is willing to take both on approval until a decision can be reached."

– Mary Day Winn

My Secret Weapon

Chapter Seven
Using The Weapon

The third dimension of modesty, as mentioned earlier, is dressing up the power. This dimension is the most charged issue in the discussion of modesty because it gives instructions on what women should and should not wear. Much has been written about how Christian women should dress. And much of what is written is focused on hemlines, necklines, and religious lines. While I will cover the familiar territory of hemlines, necklines, and religious lines, my major concern is how a woman uses the most prominent aspect of her powerful weapon.

Modesty was not a discussion when man was created. When Adam and Eve came from the hand of the Creator, they were covered in His glory. But something happened. "Then the Lord God called to Adam and said to him, 'Where are you?' So he said, I heard Your voice in the garden, and I was afraid because I was naked; and I hid myself.' And He said, 'Who told you that you were naked? Have you eaten from the tree of which I commanded you that you should not eat?' To which Adam replied, "The woman whom You gave to be with me, she gave me of the tree, and I ate." (Genesis 3:9-12) The statement by Adam, "I was afraid because I was naked," began the sensitive discussion about modesty. It is the first record of a woman's power and the first account of the explosive misuse of the feminine power, the weapon. Although we know about the verbal exchange that transpired between the serpent and Eve in regard to eating from the forbidden tree, we do not have a record of the conversation that took place between Adam and Eve. What we have is a record of what happened. "So when the woman saw that the tree was good for food, that it was pleasant to the eyes, and a tree desirable to make one wise, she took of its fruit and ate. She also gave to her husband with her, and he ate" (Genesis 3:6). Adam ate the fruit that his wife gave to him anyway, even after they were told not to touch the fruit because they would surely die (Genesis 2:17). Wow, the power of a woman! Adam was willing to exchange eternal life to please his beautiful wife.

After Adam and Eve satisfied their appetites on the forbidden fruit, their eyes were opened. They saw themselves as naked for the first time. Their first frightened instinct was to cover up. The Bible says they sewed fig leaves together to cover themselves. This partial cover-up apparently was not enough, because when God appeared and discovered them hiding, He responded to their shame. "Also for Adam and his wife the Lord God made tunics of skin, and clothed them" (Genesis 3:21). The fig leaves covered them partially, but the tunics covered them completely.

Contrary to popular opinion, the discussion of modesty is not Victorian. It originated in the Garden not long after creation. Sin stripped the first couple of their covering, re-quiring a cover-up. There is much debate surrounding a clear definition of modesty. But first understand, modesty is not a social construct.[1] If that were the case, this book, *My Secret Weapon*, would be unnecessary. Modesty means to cover yourself. It is not something that is defined by a community, but it is shaped in community. And since the fall, after the covering of God was lost, there has been a need by both men and women to cover up – to be modest. Covering up holds especially true for women, with our explosive inner power. We manage our powerful weapons by dressing them up.

I believe that one of the most profound ways that we women demonstrate the responsible use of our weapon is through dress. Yes, our dress. Through our dress, we are able to exhibit our power, our being, who we are. What we dress our bodies in and how we wear what we put on our bodies, communicates our values. "Clothing does not just drape the flesh but extends it. Clothing reveals personal ambitions, social aspirations, and the prevailing zeitgeist (the spirit of the times)."[2]

After years of struggling with the sensitive issues of modesty, I found a common sense approach to using our secret weapon responsibly. My major concern in this discussion is to help you know and understand that you are powerful; that the responsible use of your weapon doesn't take away your power but increases your power. This is the nuts and bolts of using your weapon. In this section, I will discuss the power women have through their dress and the role that fashion plays in how women use that power.

Megatrends for Women illustrates the power women have in the world. It shows how women are the catalysts through which major change occurs in our world. The book chronicles how women are the critical mass for the changes we see in politics, sports, the workplace, and religion.[3] It is however, through fashion – what a woman chooses to wear – that she can exhort, use, and demonstrate her explosive inner power. Although some women may consider buying clothes a leisure activity, it is the vehicle through which a woman exercises her power, her *being*.

Women begin to exert their power early in life. A few years ago, I was teaching *Skills for Living* at a middle school in a suburban area. I enjoyed teaching the class. I felt privileged to work with students during a very critical period in their lives. I was passionate about the subject because I was preparing students to become productive, responsible adults in the areas of family, health, finance, and career. On Fridays, we would have Discovery Days. The students would come to class prepared to do a variety of activities, including food preparation relays as well as dusting and cleaning the room. While the class was fun and exciting, one of the challenges was enforcing the school's dress code. The students were required to wear uniforms. The rules were clear: shirt tails tucked in, no sagging, no bagging, no low necklines for the girls. Like most children at that age, they did not like wearing the uniforms. They did not like following the rules. As a caring teacher, one of my primary concerns was showing students how following school rules was transferable into adult life. One of the rules that I persistently enforced with the girls was the "no low neckline rule." The girls would come to class wearing their uniform shirts unbuttoned. This was not as distracting with the girls that had "raisins" (as my daughter called them) or plum-sized breasts. However, when the girls with fully developed large breasts walked into the class with their blouses unbuttoned, it caused a different response. This was especially true of one girl who wore her blouse unbuttoned and sometimes revealed an extremely low neckline. Her voluptuous breasts would bounce around like two bowling balls, causing eyestrain for the boys. One day, using as much tact as possible, I asked her to come behind my desk so she could look into the mirror that hung suspended at eye level. I wanted her to see what everyone else was seeing. Having students look at themselves in the mirror at this age is the same as giving them a candy bar. During adolescence, boys and girls become intensely concerned with their looks. The young lady's response was no surprise to me as she stood looking into the mirror. She looked at her hair from one side, and then she turned to see the other side. Then I prodded, "Now tell me, what do you see?" I really do not know why I thought for even one second that I could get a hormone-raging thirteen-year-old girl to say, "Oh, Dr. Hill, I am showing too much cleavage." I was mistaken. I had to help her out by bringing to her attention her exposed cleavage, the space between her breasts. Her response to me was simple – "But Miss, it's the style." She did not know that even at her age she possessed power that could change the boys' focus in class from the bread recipes to her breasts. What she did know is that the attention she received made her feel good. But what she did not know was that the boys in her class were beginning to notice the differences between males and females. During puberty, boys and girls experience increased levels of testosterone (the male hormone) and estrogen (the female hormone). "However the rate of increase is gender-specific: Testosterone production skyrockets in boys, up to 18 times the level in childhood, but increases much less in girls. Estrogen production increases up to eight times in girls."[4] I told her that the boys were going to continue to look at her breasts if she exposed them because it was natural for them to do so. I asked her what she wanted to communicate about herself through her dress. She had not given it any thought. However, I noticed after our talk, from that day on, whenever she came to my class her blouse was buttoned up, and no peeks into her valley were visible, even if it meant pressing a folder against her chest while sitting in the classroom.

I wish I could say that was just the response of an adolescent, but many women also say, "Well, that's the style." Or, "Everybody's wearing it." These statements made by women remind me of the caricature of the young mallard duck that came home with his bill turned around backwards. His mom was furious. Looking at him, one could read her thoughts by her facial expression – "Do you see how despicable you look?" After reading his mom's facial expressions, the son responded, "But mom, everybody's wearing the bill in the back!" Keeping up with the latest fashion trends holds true for adults as well as adolescents. It is estimated that women spend five times as much as men do on clothing. Liz Clayborne generates almost four times the women's clothing sales of the top three male designers combined.[5] The question to ask yourself is, Should I buy clothes just to be fashionable? Falling into the fashion trap is like letting someone else write your résumé. One common sense approach to buying fashion is to know that the latest fashion trends typically are overpriced and shoddy.[6]

> "Fashion is a woman's ready muse in the quest for self-expression. It is her wardrobe mistress in the drama of corporate success. But if fashion is to support a woman's success and satisfaction, it must come from the inside out. When a woman's clothing accurately reflects her taste and style and flatters her body type, something clicks psychologically. She feels empowered to take on the world."[7]

I know how I feel whenever I step out wearing a new outfit or one of my favorite ensembles, not to mention when I've just returned from the hair salon and have gotten a facial – Watch out world, here I come! I feel like one woman business owner who said to me, "I'm large and in charge." As God's extraordinary creation, women must stop and think before selecting something that is fashionable. So the simple common sense rule about following fashion: Stop it. Stop following fashion. Write your own résumé.

I remember talking with a friend after one of my presentations on *My Secret Weapon*. She apologized to me for not attending my presentation because she was told that it was about *how* to dress and she already knew how to do that. Sadly, she missed the premise of the discussion. *My Secret Weapon*, the seminar presentation and the book, are more than about *how* to dress. It is really more about the awareness of your *being*. It's about the power that we have been given as women. And it's also about using that power responsibly. Because dress is an important component in the daily lives of women, I use the discussion of dress to show how it relates to the awesome power of a woman. Part of the message we send about who we are when we go out is sent by what we wear.

I really appreciate John Molloy's work in his two books entitled *Dress for Success for Women* and the *New Women's Dress for Success*. Although his research speaks mainly to the role of dress in the workplace, I believe that Christian women can also use the principles he outlines in their everyday lives. For example, Molloy indicated that most women dressed for failure. However, the fact that a woman may know what to wear does not guarantee success in the workplace. "Research shows that when a woman dresses for success, it does not guarantee success, but if she dresses poorly, or inappropriately, it almost always ensures failure."[8] As important as dress is, if a man dresses poorly, it does not destroy his career the way it does a woman. He can be considered as "a diamond in the rough" and he will be promoted despite having a poor image. Often, a man will be told that he is not dressed appropriately. And Molloy further states, "A woman who dresses inappropriately, she will be eliminated from consideration for management by most men and women managers."[9] Many times, her male boss will not let her know that she is inappropriately dressed because it would be considered politically incorrect. On the other hand, a woman superior finds it difficult as well, because she feels that it is not her job to tell a woman that she is not dressed appropriately. What I am talking about here goes deeper than how to dress. By now you should know that dress is simply a way to communicate to others about your *being*, who you are. It is through clothing that women express who they are, as well as their place in society.

A couple of years ago I was taking a tour of the Capitol building. I was given instructions about the appropriate dress that I would have to wear in order to obtain entrance into the building. I was told that my attire had to be a business suit with dark colors, no exposed legs (all the women had to wear pantyhose), and no exposed arms were allowed. This requirement intrigued and amazed me because I was being asked to do all this, even though I was not going to see the president, nor was I even physically going into the White House. I was going into one of the buildings on Capitol Hill.

On another occasion, it was my turn to do my civic duty and serve as a juror on a criminal case. I had managed to avoid going to jury duty multiple times before, because I had young children at home, or I was a full-time student and could opt out of serving. This time I could not get out of it. So I had to go. Again, I received specific guidelines for my attire — no short skirts, short sleeves, or provocative clothing. This really alerted me again to the importance of dress, and women's dress in particular. As a believer, what attire should I choose to wear when I go to church, to worship the Most High God? Should I have a lower standard for God's house than is required for the White House or the courthouse? Sadly, the standard for God's house appears to be lower. I believe this is the case because we have not taken time to teach women about their inner explosive power and how to use it responsibly. I believe that women fall into one of the following categories when it comes to knowing about their secret weapon: Some women have no clue, no idea that they are such powerful beings; some women know that they are powerful, but they do not know how use their power responsibly; others know and understand full well that they have this explosive inner power yet choose to use it irresponsibly. I tend to believe that a lot of women fall into the first category – they just don't know or understand that God made them as powerful as they are.

While writing this book, I saw an interview with a young female performer. She is not just famous in this country but throughout the world. This feminine dynamo measures up to her fame on all fronts. She is all the media has made her to be and more. She grew up middle class, in a Christian home, free from drugs and alcohol. Today, she is a multi Grammy Award-winning artist. In the interview, this celebrity performer stated that she prays before stepping out on stage prior to each performance. She's got it all; she is beautiful, she's talented, and she's rich. But I was caught off-guard by two profound statements from her interview. First, the interviewer made comments about her great upbringing and then said, "But you are known as a seductress," to which she quickly replied, "I'll take that." I really thought that I missed the definition of the word because she took it as a compliment. I went to my dictionary and looked up the word and found that it means, "one who seduces." The second statement that caught my attention was that this woman is known as the symbol of female empowerment. Since most of her followers are women, she is exerting her power and it is having an enormous impact. This female artist exemplifies what many women are seeking to become. Young girls and older women want to be like her, they want to look like her, and they want to dress like her. Now, that's extreme power. But listen, as the voice for feminine responsible living, I am speaking up. I will be like the little boy in the fairy tale entitled "The Emperor's New Clothes," who spoke out in the parade when the emperor was being carried through the streets in what he thought was a beautiful, expensive, finely made robe and said, "He's naked, he doesn't have any clothes on." This famous Grammy Award-winning artist is naked "She doesn't have enough clothes on." And nobody really wants to say it. Yes, this young woman is very talented. It bears repeating. She is very beautiful. She is more powerful than she knows. However, she is influencing many women through her feminine power to think that to become famous, to be beautiful, to make money, you must expose yourself. I truly believe she would be better to herself if she understood *who* she is; if she knew her identity as a daughter of the Most High God; if she knew that she was created to bring glory to God. I wish she knew all of that and would then unequivocally commit to using her explosive inner power and talents to honor and glorify God. Wow, she would be totally awesome! Enough said.

I've listened to compliments given by women to women. The words, "That outfit makes you look appealing," or "You are HOT," appear to make the receiver feel complete. What does that mean to you when someone makes such a statement to you? How does it make you feel when someone tells you that you are appealing? Well, I took the liberty of asking a college sophomore who was seated next to me on the airplane as I returned home from the annual National Council on Family Relations Conference. I noticed that she was looking at a magazine entitled *Allure*. Since I was writing my book, it seemed fitting for me to get her opinion about the magazine and why she was so drawn to it. She proceeded to tell me that she liked dressing up and looking pretty. However, she mentioned that she would not dare wear a dress that would be short in length and show her cleavage at the same time. She would only do one or the other, but never both. I asked her, "Why not?" She responded, "It would be too much for me to do both." She would wear a short dress with no cleavage or show cleavage wearing a long dress, but never the two at the same time. Pointing to one of women in the magazine, she said, " I feel appealing when I wear a dress like this." To which I asked, "What do you mean, you feel appealing?" She thought for a second, and then responded, "I feel special." An "Aha" moment flashed for me. It all made more sense to me why some women go out revealing their secret weapon. Perhaps, they, too, want to feel special, be noticed, and maybe even feel "loved" by someone.

As a woman of God, you must stop and think before selecting something that is fashionable to wear. You must be mindful that you are always communicating who you are through your dress. It is the place where you as a woman exercise your power, your *being*. What are you communicating? In the next chapter, I want to share with you my five Secret Weapon Tests. These tests are designed to help you determine whether or not you are using your explosive inner power responsibly.

My Secret Weapon

Chapter Eight

Testing The Weapon

"Women have explosive inner power. We didn't earn it. We didn't purchase it. We don't even deserve it. It is our birthright as daughters of God. It is a God-gift that can't be destroyed or denied."

– Dr. Susie M. Hill

My Secret Weapon

My Secret Weapon
Test One

Headlights Beaming

Can you see your headlights beaming through your dress, blouse, or shirt? If so, your garment is too sheer or too tight.

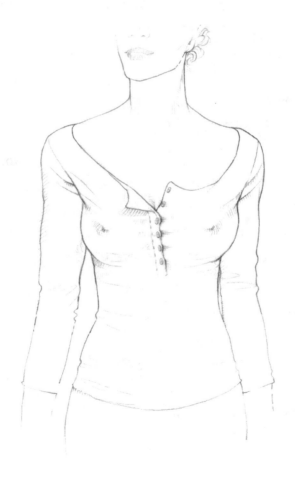

Much of what has been discussed in my book is the *being* of a woman. I've sought to be clear that modesty is more about the *being*, not the *doing*. However, before unlocking the secret weapon, I must add that the doing of modesty is found in the Secret Weapon Tests. Your actions are the true test of who you are. So now take the Headlights Beaming test as named by a friend of mine, Nicole Pruitt. Look in the mirror and see if you can see your "headlights" beaming through. Can you see the contour of your breasts in the mirror? If so, then your blouse, dress, or T-shirt is too tight. If the contour of your breasts is easily identifiable, then you are putting your light bulbs out there front and center. Usually, clothing made of Fish Chale and fine metallic knits, Lycra, Spandex, rayon, silk jersey, or ultra-fine closely-fit knits[1] will reveal your secret weapon with one flash of the light bulbs.

"In each segment of history, fashion indeed singles out some section of the female skin as sensuous."[2] It appears that accenting a woman's breasts has become very fashionable. I was having dinner after church with some family members on one of our out-of-town trips. I mentioned how I was seated in the rear section of the church and was not able to get a good glimpse of the soloist unless I looked on the large projection video screen. The young woman was singing one of my favorite songs, "We Shall Behold Him." I was envisioning myself signing to this majestic song that moves people to tears at the thought of seeing Jesus face-to-face. My sentiments shifted a bit as I looked up at the screen and the soloist bellowed out, 'We Shall Beholddddd Himmmm, Yes, We Shall, Beholdddd Himm…," when to my surprise, I noticed that the singer's nipples were at attention, piercing through her fishnet-lined dress. I was oblivious that my father-in-law was there at the dinner table listening. With his eyes closed, he replied, "You mean she was signing, "We Shall Behold THEM……" That's really what happens when we wear shear, thin, translucent fabrics. When women get excited or cold, it is perfectly normal to get "nipply." It does not just happen when we are aroused. This happens when the garment is so thin that it puts everyone on notice. If you can see through your clothing, chances are that others can too. If the contour of your breasts can be easily identified, then you are exposing enough for the missing parts to be completed. Fashion designers have created garments for women to wear from diaphanous materials. These are transparent materials and fabrics that allow one to see through them.

Not only are transparent fabrics keeping women from guarding their secret weapon, but they can also become problematic when they fit tightly. I must say that *Tight Is*

Not Right – not only does everything that a woman wears send a message, but how she wears her clothing sends a message.

Here is what some men said in response to a survey of Christian Men on the Subject of Women's Clothing:[3]

"Tight clothing is at least as much a potential problem for men as skimpy clothing."

"I would say the number-one problem is any garment that is form-fitting, be it jeans, pants, skirt, dress, shirt, whatever. Anything that is tight, no matter how long it is, leaves nothing to the imagination, and that defeats the whole purpose of covering the skin in the first place!"

"You don't even need to see skin; they (tight clothing) provide all the curves."

"The point is that it is not the type of clothing that can trip a man up, rather, it is the amount and level of cling to the body."

Chapter Eight

Solution

Be encouraged! You don't have to give up style in order to look beautiful. The transparent materials do pose a challenge if you are trying to guard your secret weapon. I have found that layering works well if the layers being used are not made of the same Fish Chale and fine fabrics. Look for the better natural fibers when shopping. They will serve you well and last longer than some of the synthetic fabrics. If your outfit is sheer, you will need to dress in multiple layers in order to avoid misusing your secret weapon. Scarves, jackets, and vests are a great way to accessorize and can also serve as a protective shield for you. But of course, if your outfit is too tight, it is a no-brainer; either you shed some of those extra pounds, or you will need to go and get the next size up to avoid looking like stuffing for the turkey. I also recommend that you use the mirror, or you may even ask a girlfriend to help you guard your secret weapon. If all else fails, I like what Mark Twain said, "When in doubt, strike it out."

My Secret Weapon
Test Two

Cheeks
Can You See My Cheeks?

The only cheeks that a woman of God should be showing in public are the ones on her face.

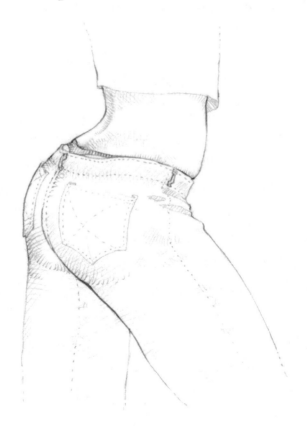

Yes, the only cheeks that a woman of God should be showing in public are the ones on her face. Yet, all types and sizes of cheeks are being exposed today, and that amazes me. Please note: fashion designers dictate this overexposure of cheeks.

My sister-in-law was attending a fashion show where the designers were showcasing the next season's fashions. She told me about the response of a gentleman who was seated near her as the grand finale outfit was being showcased. The model strutted down the catwalk toward the spectators, and with her precisioned walk, she stopped, pivoted, and with a jolt, turned in front of an unsuspecting gentleman. She gave him an up-close-and-personal display of her uncovered rear cheeks, right in his face. Although the model flashed her cheeks for just a few short seconds, in a desperate but sincere outburst, the gentleman cried out, "OH LORD, WHAT DO YOU WANT ME TO DO NOW?" He was being pulled by the powerful magnetic force of a woman he did not even know. Now you know that's POWER!

A gentleman went to his pastor and pleaded with him saying, "Pastor, can you please talk to the women of the church? Please tell them to cover up. We are bombarded all week long with sensual images as we go back and forth to work, as we watch television. It's everywhere. We come

116

to church expecting to find a safe place, a place that is free from the seductive images that attack us every single day. Then when we come to church and we see that the women in church are dressing no differently than what is out there. It makes it hard for us as men who are trying to keep our minds from wandering. Please, please tell them to cover up!" Well, I don't know if you want your pastor telling you to cover up. He should not have to do that. But pastors on occasion have had to speak to the issue. I heard of a pastor who asked a single young woman to stop wearing her extremely short dresses, especially when serving before the congregation. Apparently, the young lady was offended by the gentle request and shortly afterward, in protest, wore a short dress while telling the children's story. The story was well done but she had to remain in an upright position to avoid losing her explosive inner power. Shortly thereafter, she stopped attending that church and moved to another.

Although women may not be baring their literal cheeks in public, some of the styles are designed to give an epiphany of flesh. The amazing thing is that a lot of people are telling others as they did in "The Emperor's New Clothes," that they look good. But the truth is, many women are exposing themselves. Like me, Shannon Rupp, a global researcher, is one who is not caught up in "The Emperor's New Clothes" syndrome. She talks straight about what these fashion trends do and how they impact the power of a woman. She points out that, "Butt-baring jeans rob women of power. Aside from telegraphing that she sees herself as a member of a social underclass, just how much authority can any woman claim when she is preoccupied with yanking her trousers?"[1]

Solution

Shop for pants that have the full cut in style. They can be found. If you still have some pants in your closet that show your rear checks, simply wear a top to cover the entire territory. Yes, you must cover the entire territory; all of what God gave you. You were designed to intoxicate just one man (your husband) with your power gift, not every man.

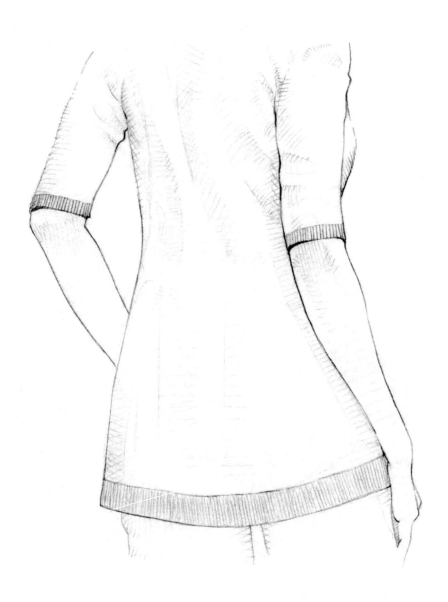

My Secret Weapon
Test Three

Pit-Stop
Are my sleeves too short?

If we can see your underarm pits, then you are revealing too much skin.

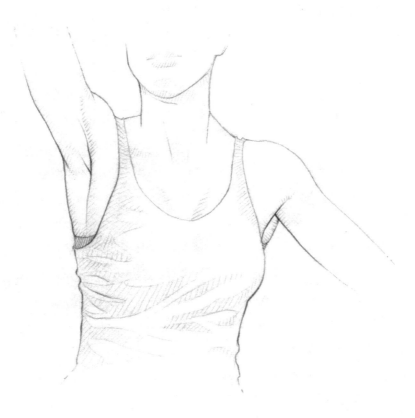

Modesty means to cover up. Yes, I know that this sounds old-fashioned. But women who are concerned with using their secret weapon responsibly don't mind being old-fashioned. That is, old-fashioned in values, not fashion. I'm glad for some of the changes that have occurred in fashion. I don't think that I would enjoy wearing the dresses that were fashionable during the 1800s that weighed, by some estimation, as much as nine pounds. But it is alarming to see the drastic changes in fashion designed to strike a deathblow to modesty. Don't overlook the Public Undressing of America 1890s – 2000s list I have included that historically accounts for the disrobing of America. We have moved from covering every part of the human body to exposing everything. Just recently, a gentleman was attending a funeral service at a large church. He leaned over to the person sitting next to him and said, "It is so nice to see the choir wearing their robes. We don't have to be bombarded with those underarm pits." It entices some men when they can view the northern region and it reminds them of the southern region. It is also amazing to me how many women have such high self-confidence that they leave home exposing their underarm pits, no matter the size of their biceps. I always ask, "Why would you do that to America?"

An e-mail was sent to participants of a large gathering of

women pertaining to the expected dress code. In the e-mail, the director confessed apologetically the struggle she faced with presenters and their dress. It read: "I know it isn't necessary, but please bear with me for mentioning dress guidelines for those on the rostrum and conducting seminars during the convention: 1) Skirts/dresses should cover the knees when standing and sitting. 2) Cleavage is a no-no. Please make sure your top is high enough that even if you lean over or the top rides down, it won't show cleavage. 3). Bare shoulders are also inappropriate." Women from all around the world attended the convention and the presence of the Lord was seen and felt throughout the entire event. Not one dry eye was seen at the end of the closing service of the convention. But one of the young participants either did not get the e-mail message or just chose not to heed the instructions. She had on a beautiful sleeveless top that revealed her underarm pits each time she stretched out her arms. Her heart was in her performance but we were distracted as we were lured into her "pit stop."

Solution

Let's just make this one easy: If you are going to face the public, whether it is work, church, or business, wear sleeves. I was given this regulation going to serve as a juror, and on my visit to the Capitol building. You want to consider the "no pit-stop" regulation when speaker or presenting in a public gathering.

My Secret Weapon

My Secret Weapon
Test Four

Palm Pilot
Is my blouse or my dress too low?[1]

*If you can see the valley between your breasts,
then your blouse or dress is too low.*

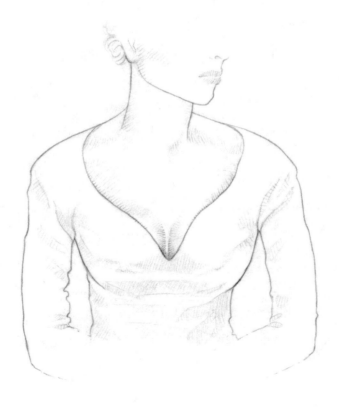

It's called cleavage, the valley between your breasts. If your cleavage can be seen, then you are having what I call "an epiphany of female flesh." And that's not good. Modesty requires your cleavage to be covered. Think about this song when your cleavage is showing: "Down in the valley, the valley so low, hang your head over, let the wind blow." If the valley is visible, then the men will certainly have a place to hang their heads. This statement gives insight into what happens to men when cleavage is shown: "Men admired, feared, revered, and stared at a woman's upfront prominence. Her breasts, the source of ever-flowing nourishment, constituted her power."[2] While showing cleavage has become fashionable for women, both young and old, it is still not modest. It appears that there is an epidemic of women of God that are failing this Secret Weapon Test. It really struck a chord with me as I drove onto the parking lot of a very large church. The parking lot was so large a shuttle service was provided. As I watched the women who boarded the shuttle and those who walked, I noticed that "cleavage" appeared to be the dress code of the day. I have been to numerous churches across the country, but this one received the Emmy Award for "Leaving it to Cleavage." Old, young, round, and bound women were failing the Palm Pilot test. One young woman had a split in her dress right down her valley, almost to her navel, and the same length split was repeated in the back. The epiphany of female flesh communicates loudly a woman's values.

Solution

Avoid the safety pin approach. A safety pin changes the structure of your outfit. It creates a pucker that becomes an eyesore, drawing even more attention. Instead, try draping or tying a scarf around the open area. A scarf can be a great way to complement an outfit and keep you from failing the Palm Pilot test. A nice shell under your top or dress can also serve to completely cover the valley. Just make sure that it does not look like underwear parading as outerwear. Better still, choose outfits that don't show cleavage.

My Secret Weapon
Test Five

Intended Use Rule

When selecting your clothing, it is important to consider the intended use of the garment.

It was in the 1980s when designers in the fashion industry started using undergarments as outerwear. While she was not the first to wear underwear as outerwear, Madonna is credited for bringing the use of undergarments as outerwear to the masses and popularizing it. It was through the use of this fashion that the material girl, Madonna, used her secret weapon, her power, as an expression of a woman's feminine freedom.[1] She made it fashionable to wear the leggings that were finished with lace at the bottom. Until then, women wore this garment under their petticoats. During the Victorian era, it was alluring for a woman to show her ankle. Today all parts of the feminine flesh are exposed. The fabrics that were once only used to make sleepwear or underwear are being paraded on the catwalk and the department stores as outerwear. When selecting your wardrobe, consider its intended use: Is it for work, home, bed, or recreation? The setting should determine the garment. It sounds simple, but women are still wearing garments to the workplace that were originally designed as lingerie.

I remember when it became fashionable for girls to wear their house slippers to school. You would see girls walking through the halls in their pink, bunny rabbit house slippers. The school districts had to rewrite the school dress code policy to help students know what to wear.

Don't rewrite the rules. Remember the Intended Use Rule.

"Also, I wish that our members especially the women, would dress modestly (covered up, not exposing themselves), sensibly and in harmony with what is proper for Christian decency and dignity. They should not draw attention to themselves by such things as outlandish hairdos, gaudy makeup, ornaments of gold or pearls and expensive clothes like pagan worshipers do."

–1 Timothy 2:9, The Clear Word

My Secret Weapon

Chapter Nine
My Secret Weapon Unlocked

What is "my secret weapon?" Have you figured it out yet? Well, it's a secret, and that is why I intentionally waited to the end to reveal it. I needed to lay a foundation and frame the discussion before I could divulge "my secret weapon." I wanted you to know its origins and its power. I wanted you to know its true value and importance. I wanted you to be convinced that "my secret weapon" is worth keeping a secret. I wanted you to sense the urgency of using "my secret weapon" with wisdom and grace. As the voice for feminine responsible living, I see the great need for women to discover their secret weapon. Too many women, young and old, are unaware of their secret weapon and the few that are aware struggle to use it responsibly. So, are you ready? Look in the box on the next page and decipher the coded letters.

The Secret Weapon is your sexuality. Don't confuse sexuality with sexual intimacy. The word sexuality refers to your being. Sexuality is who you are – a woman. Your sexuality is your explosive inner power covered in feminine allurement. It's your curves and your core. The root word in sexuality is sex. Do you know the definition of sex? Most people don't know the meaning, thus the confusion about the secret weapon. The primary meaning of the word sex is gender. It means male or female.

Simply put, your secret weapon is who you are — a woman who is powerful, a woman who is beautiful, created in the image of an awesome God. This awesome explosive inner power sets you apart. Remember, we didn't earn it.

We didn't purchase it. We don't even deserve it. It is our birthright as daughters of God. It is a God-gift that can't be destroyed or denied. Use your gift as God intended for you to use it: to bring honor and glory to His name and bless others. Using your secret weapon is a call to walking closer with God. It is a call to order your life in His Word. So, I commission you to use your power responsibly. You have a right to feel special – because you are. You will be noticed because that's what the power does – it causes others to notice you. Your secret weapon becomes unlocked when you recognize your explosive inner power and decide to use it responsibly. Remember, a weapon is an instrument designed to inflict injury or death to an opponent or to defend, protect, or rescue the individual, friend, or companion. It is an instrument that can be used for good or evil. With your secret weapon now unlocked, you are now one armed and dangerous woman for God. Go and change your world. Start by writing your own feminine résumé.

My Secret Weapon

Chapter Ten
Write Your Own Feminine Résumé

Do you know who you are? Are you certain about your identity? You should by now know who you are because your identity is a consistent definition of your self as a unique individual, in terms of roles, attitudes, beliefs, and aspirations.[1] Once you have defined your "goals, values, and beliefs and you have unequivocally committed to them, it gives you a sense of direction, meaning, and purpose to life."[2] If you allow the fashion industry to influence what you wear, it's like letting a stranger write your résumé.[3] Take charge of your feminine identity by writing your own résumé. Fashion involves more than simply imitating another person's style. It is a form of nonverbal communication that provides a way for people to express their identities and values."[4]

Feminine Identity Components

Begin writing your feminine identity statement by simply writing down what you see as the most important things in your life: God, family, honesty, education, etc. Then make a declaration that when you step out into the world, you look like the values you have committed to and that you will be true to your own feminine identity statement.

1. _____

2. _____

3. _____

4. _____

5. _____

6. _____

7. _____

My Feminine Identity Statement

As a daughter of God, I recognize the love my heavenly Father has for me because He created me to walk in paths I do not know, requiring me to trust and believe that His way is best for me.

Genesis 1:26, 27; Ephesians 2:10; Philippians 1:6

Personal Impact Feminine Identity Statement

God has called me as a wife, mother, grandmother, and friend, to educate and motivate Christian women about the powerful gift He has given them. This calling by God to be "the voice for feminine responsible living," will be carried by way of public speaking, teaching seminars, and writing publications. Using a three-tier formula that combines theology, social theory, and a common-sense approach I will release women to use their feminine power responsibly as they walk in their God-calling. This will be evident when women accept their position as daughters of God and use their feminine power to change the world around them.

– Dr. Susie M. Hill – The Voice For
Feminine Responsible Living

My Secret Weapon

"Clothing does not just drape the flesh but extends it. Clothing reveals personal ambitions, social aspirations, and the prevailing zeitgeist (the spirit of the times)."

– Richard J. Alapack

Fashion Facts
The Public Undressing of America*

1890s – Swimwear was modified street clothing.

1910s – Arms were exposed.

1920s – You would be arrested if you appeared in a modest twenty-first century bathing suit; legs and backs were exposed.

1930s – Cleavage was exposed and men began to swim bare-chested. Two-piece bathing suits appeared with a small break between upper and lower half.

1940s – New fabrics appeared that hugged the body.

1960s – Navels were exposed; women took off their bras.

1970s – Legs were exposed through mini and micro-mini shorts.

1980s – Underwear was worn as outerwear.

1990s – The decade of "anti-fashion." Retro clothes from 1960s and 1970s.

2000s – Belly buttons, cleavage, legs, buttocks were showing. Is there anything left?

*Jeff Pollard, *Christian Modesty and the Public Undressing of America* (2004).

Endnotes

Introduction

1. Ellen G. White, *The Adventist Home* (Washington DC: Review and Herald, 1952), p. 231.
2. Gail Collins, *America's Women* (New York: HarperCollins, 2003), p. 49.
3. Howard V. Hayghe, "Developments in Women's Labor Force Participation," *Monthly Labor Review* (September 1997), p. 42.
4. Judith Hennessee, *Betty Friedan Her Life* (New York: Random House, 1999).
5. Betty Freidan, *The Feminine Mystique* (New York: Norton, 1997).
6. Collins, *America's Women*, p. 49.
7. Richard J. Alapack, "The Epiphany of Female Flesh: A Feminist Goal to Shed Light on Women/Phenomenological Hermeneutic of Popular Fashion," *The Journal of Popular Culture* 46, No. 6 (2009), p. 994.

Chapter One

1. White, *The Adventist Home*, p. 231.

Chapter Two

1. Tamar El-Or, "The Length of Slits and the Spread of Luxury: Reconstructing the Subordination of Ultra-Orthodox Jewish Women Through the Patriarch of Men Scholars," *Sex Roles* 29, no. 9/10 (1993).

Chapter Five

1. Earl Babbie, *The Practice of Social Research* 10th ed. (Belmont, CA: Thomson Wadsworth, 2004), p. 30.
2. Patricia Aburdene and John Naisbitt, *Megatrends for Women* (New York: Villard Books, 2000), p. 265.
3. Marie Withers Osmond and Barrie Thorne, "Feminists Theories: The Social Construction of Gender in Families

and Society," In *Sourcebook of Family Theories and Methods: A Conceptual Approach.* (Ed.) Pauline Boss, William J. Doherty, Ralph LaRossa, Walter R. Schumm, and Suzanne K. Steinmetz, (New York: Plenum Press, 1993), p. 591.

4. Aburdene, and Naisbitt, *Megatrends for Women*, p. 265.
5. Alapack, "The Epiphany of Female Flesh," p. 977.
6. Margaret A. Lowe, "From Robust Appetites to Calorie Counting: The Emergence of Dieting Among Smith College Students in the 1920s," *Journal of Women's History* 7, no. 4 (1995), p. 111.
7. Kendra Cleave, "Fashioning the College Woman: Dress, Gender, and Sexuality at Smith College in the 1920s," *The Journal of American Culture* 32, no. 1 (2009), p. 4.
8. Ibid, p.7.
9. Greg Kearsley, Explorations in Learning and Instructions: The Theory Into Practice Database: Gestalt Theory. George Washington University. Available at http://www.alokjain.pbworks.com/GestaltTheory [1/22/2010].
10. The Museum at FIT, "Seduction – 250 Years of Sexuality in Fashion," (October 29, 2008). Available at http:www.fitnyc.edu/museum [1/25/2010].
11. Alapack, "The Epiphany of Female Flesh," p. 978.
12. http://www.fitnyc.edu/musuem
13. Gary M. Yontef, *Awareness, Dialogue, and Process, Essays on Gestalt Therapy* (Highland, NY: Gestalt Journal Press, 1993).
14. Dannah Gresh, *Secret Keeper: The Delicate Power of Modesty* (Chicago: Moody Publishers, (2002), p. 19.
15. Kendra Cleave, "Fashioning the College Woman: Dress, Gender, and Sexuality at Smith College in the 1920s," *The Journal of American Culture* 32 (March 2009), p. 6.
16. Ibid., p. 13.
17. John T. Molloy, *New Dress for Success for Women* (New York: Business Plus, 1996).
18. Maurice Merleau-Ponty, *The Phenomenology of Perception* (London: Routledge & Kegan, 1962).

19. Alapack, "The Epiphany of Female Flesh," p. 977.
20. James T. Saw, 2D Design Notes, Art 104: Design Composition, 2000, available at http://daphne.palomar.edu/desin/gestalt.html [8/19/2009]. Used by permission.
21. Gresh, *Secret Keeper*, p. 45.
22. Debbie Jensen, Law of Continuation, available at http://ezinerArticles.com/?expert-Debbiee.Jensen, [2/23/2010].

Chapter Six
1. Williston Walker, *A History of the Christian Church* (New York: Charles Scribner & Sons, 1958), p.52.
2. Henry Chadwick, *The Early Church* (London: Cox & Wyman, 1967), p. 286.
3. Jack Canfield, et al., "Behind Every Great Man Is a Great Woman," *Chicken Soup for the Couple's Soul* (Deerfield Beach, FL: Health Communications, 1999), pp. 167, 168.
4. United Jewish Communities, National Women's Philanthropy, available at http://www.JewishFederation.org [2/25/2010].
5. Christine Rose, "Church Ladies: Women Dominate America's Pews. Is that a Problem?," The Wall Street Journal, October 21, 2005, www.opinionjournal.com/taste/?id=110007439, [4/28/10].
6. Ben D. Kennedy, Maid of Heaven (Louisville, KY: RLK Press, 2007).

Chapter Seven
1. Wendy Shalit, "Proud to Be Modest," *Christianity Today* 44 (January 2000), p. 70.
2. Alapack, "The Epiphany of Female Flesh," p. 977.
3. Aburdene and Naisbitt, *Megatrends for Women*, p. 265.
4. Robert Malina and Claude Bouchard, *Growth Maturation and Physical Activity* (Champain, IL: Human Kinetics Books, 1991).
5. Aburdene and Naisbitt, *Megatrends for Women*, p. 265.

6. Molloy, *New Women's Dress for Succes*, p. 11.
7. Aburdene and Naisbitt, *Megatrends for Women*, p. 118.
8. Molloy, *New Women's Dress for Successs*, p. xi.
9. Ibid, p. xi.

Chapter Eight
Test 1
1. Alapack, "The Epiphany of Female Flesh", p. 977.
2. Ibid., p. 977.
3. Survey of Christian Men on the Subject of Women's Clothing, Way of LIfe Literature, August 6, 2008, Available at http://www.wayoflife.org/files/335de5e4421ca77981f29f0f58c b6654-78.html [1/28/2010]

Test 2
1. Shannon Rupp, "Plumbing the History of the New Cleavage." *The Tyee.ca* 16 February 2004 http://thetyee.ca/Views/2004/02/16/Plumbing_the_History_of_the_New_Cleavage/ [1/29/2010].

Test 4
1. Gresh, *Secret Keeper*, p. 34. Used by permission.
2. Alapack, "The Epiphany of Female Flesh," p. 990.

Test 5
1. Rupp. http://thetyee.ca/Views/2004/02/16/Plumbing_the_History_of_the_New_Cleavage/.

Chapter Ten
1. Alan S. Waterman, "Finding Someone to Be: Studies on the Role of Intrinsic Motivation in Identity Formation," *Identity: An International Journal of Theory and Research* 4, no. 3 (2004), p. 209.
2. Kathleen Stassen Berger, *The Developing Person Through the Life Span*, 5th ed. (NY: Worth Publishing, 2001).
3. Molloy, *New Women's Dress for Succes*, p. 11.
4. *The Worldbook Encyclopedia* vol. 7, Fashion Chicago:Worldbook (1998).

About The Author

Dr. Susie M. Hill is a Certified Family Consumer Scientist (CFCS), a Certified Family Life Educator (CFLE), author, lecturer, keynote speaker, and consultant on family and women's issues. Dr. Hill has conducted hundreds of seminars worldwide with her husband. She is co-author of *The Financial Fitness Manual*. Dr. Hill's passion for women's issues has catapulted her to a national platform as "The Voice for Feminine Responsible Living." She is a high-energy, humorous, inspirational, bi-lingual (English and Spanish) speaker on a mission to "Preserve Families and Change Lives." She is a graduate of Andrews University, Southwestern Adventist University, and Texas Woman's University. Dr. Hill has been married to Dr. Roland J. Hill for 35 years and they have two adult children and three granddaughters.

Seminars By Dr. Susie M. Hill
Executive Summary

My Secret Weapon – Unlock the Mystery of your God-given gift. This is an intriguing and exciting approach to helping women tap into their explosive inner power.

Parenting Made Simple – Find the simpler way to raising children. Learn how to use skills that work in raising responsible adults.

Family Economics – Considers the social, psychological, and cultural factors that affect the consumer behavior of families. A powerful step-by-step guide to managing your family finances.

Intimacy, Marriage, and Money – This seminar is critical to the survival of any marriage. The presentation covers Money and Marital Intimacy, Sexuality and Money, Educating Children About Money, Budgeting, Goal Setting, Planning for Retirement, and Family Teamwork for Debt-Free Living. (Co-presentation of Drs. Roland and Susie Hill)

Theo-Economism – This seminar introduces the new cutting edge kingdom philosophy of Theo-Economism. Theo-Economism is a systematic theology of economics and stewardship designed to give believers a biblical view of God's economy. It helps believers sort out non-biblical economic philosophies that undermine their spiritual and economic potential. A must for every church member. (Co-presentation of Drs. Roland and Susie Hill)

For scheduling information, contact:
Dr. Susie M. Hill
The Voice for Feminine Responsible Living
www.drsusiehill.com
214.673.9434

The Family Life Doctors
P. O. Box 380941
Duncanville, Texas 75138
drsusiehill@sbcglobal.net